Jackals

by Jane P. Gardner

Consultant:
Blaire Van Valkenburgh
Professor
UCLA Department of Ecology and Evolutionary Biology

BEARPORT
PUBLISHING

New York, New York

Credits

Cover and Title Page, © Gerrit_de_Vries/Shutterstock; 4–5, © Clem Haagner/Science Photo Library; 6–7, 8–9, © iStockphoto/Thinkstock; 10–11, © Tish1/Shutterstock; 12–13, © imagebroker.net/SuperStock; 14, © Stu Porter/Shutterstock; 14–15, © imagebroker.net/SuperStock; 16, © Eye Ubiquitous/SuperStock; 16–17, © Hemera/Thinkstock; 18–19, © Minden Pictures/SuperStock; 20–21, © Frank Stober Image Broker/Newscom; 22T, © iStockphoto/Thinkstock; 22C, © imagebroker.net/SuperStock; 22B, © Tish1/Shutterstock; 23T, © iStockphoto/Thinkstock; 23B, © Stu Porter/Shutterstock.

Publisher: Kenn Goin
Senior Editor: Joyce Tavolacci
Creative Director: Spencer Brinker
Design: Emily Love
Photo Researcher: Arnold Ringstad

Library of Congress Cataloging-in-Publication Data

Gardner, Jane P.
  Jackals / by Jane P. Gardner.
      p. cm. — (Wild canine pups)
  Includes bibliographical references and index.
  ISBN-13: 978-1-61772-929-4 (library binding) — ISBN-10: 1-61772-929-9 (library binding)
1. Jackals—Infancy—Juvenile literature. I. Title.
  QL737.C2G37 2014
  599.77'2—dc23
                                            2013011043

For more information, write to Bearport Publishing Company, Inc., 45 West 21st Street, Suite 3B, New York, New York 10010. Printed in the United States of America.

10 9 8 7 6 5 4 3 2 1

❖ Contents ❖

Meet jackal pups 4

What is a jackal? 6

Where do jackals live? 8

A jackal family 10

Giving birth 12

Keeping safe 14

Time to eat 16

Noisy jackals 18

Growing up 20

Glossary 22

Index 24

Read more 24

Learn more online 24

About the author 24

Meet jackal pups

The sun is setting in Africa.

Three hungry jackal pups howl.

They are calling to their mother.

4

She has left the **den** to find food for them to eat.

5

What is a jackal?

Jackals are **canines**, just like dogs, foxes, and wolves.

There are three kinds of jackals.

They all have short fur and long, bushy tails.

In fact, they look like large foxes.

Adult jackal size

Where do jackals live?

Jackals live in Europe, Africa, and Asia.

Most jackals make their homes on grassy **plains** or in woods.

However, some jackals live near people in cities.

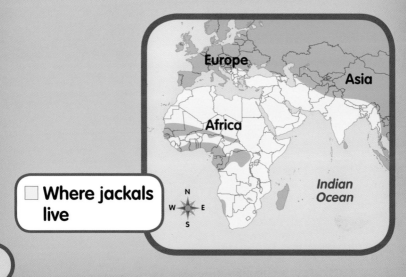

☐ **Where jackals live**

Europe

Asia

Africa

Indian Ocean

N
W — E
S

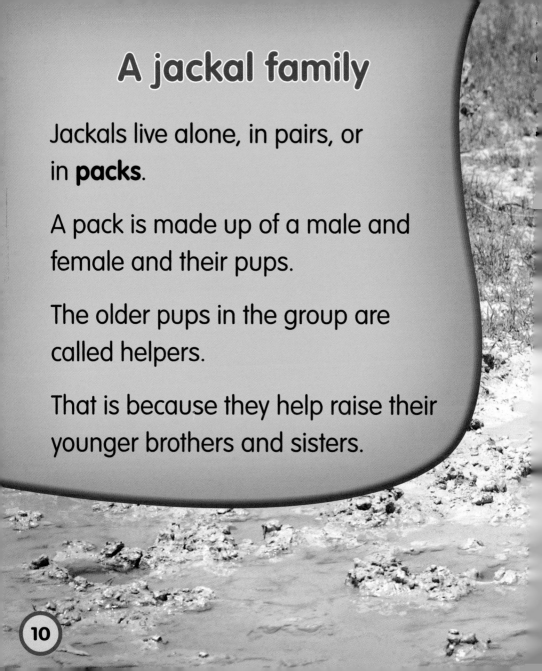

A jackal family

Jackals live alone, in pairs, or in **packs**.

A pack is made up of a male and female and their pups.

The older pups in the group are called helpers.

That is because they help raise their younger brothers and sisters.

Giving birth

A female jackal has up to seven pups in a den.

The tiny babies cannot see when they are born.

After ten days, their eyes open.

The pups stay inside the den until they are three weeks old.

Then they begin exploring outside the den.

jackal pup
in den

Keeping safe

Parents and helpers work together to keep the pups safe.

The mother jackal moves her pups to a new den every few weeks.

She does this so **predators**, such as leopards, cannot hurt the pups.

If enemies do come near, the helpers bark loudly.

leopard

This warns the pups to hide inside their den.

pups playing near den

Time to eat

At first, jackal pups drink milk from their mother's body.

When they are eight weeks old, the parents start to bring the pups meat.

The adults first chew the meat.

pups drinking milk

Then they spit it up so the pups can eat it.

To get the meat, the adults hunt small animals.

They also search for animals that are already dead.

jackal spitting up meat for pups

Noisy jackals

Jackals make many kinds of sounds.

They yell, yap, or howl to talk with each other.

Each of these sounds has a different meaning.

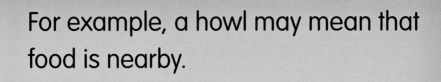

For example, a howl may mean that food is nearby.

Pups learn all these sounds by the time they are adults.

jackal pups
making noise

Growing up

Jackal pups are fully grown when they are one year old.

Some of the young animals leave to start their own pack.

However, a few stay behind to become helpers.

adult jackal with pups

They will care for their new baby brothers and sisters!

21

Glossary

canines (KAY-nyenz) members of the dog family, which includes pet dogs, wolves, and jackals

den (DEN) a home where wild animals can rest, hide from enemies, and have babies

packs (PAKS) groups of animals that live and travel together

plains (PLAYNZ) large areas filled with grass

predators (PRED-uh-turz) animals that hunt and eat other animals

Index

Africa 4, 8
Asia 8
dens 5, 12–13, 14–15
Europe 8
food 5, 16–17
fur 7

habitat 8
helpers 10, 14, 20
meat 16–17
milk 16
mothers 4–5, 10–11, 12, 14, 16

noises 4, 14–15, 18–19
packs 10, 20
plains 8
predators 14
size 6–7

Read more

Gentle, Victor. *Jackals (Wild Dogs).* Milwaukee, WI: Gareth Stevens (2002).

Gibbs, Maddie. *Jackals (Safari Animals).* New York: PowerKids Press (2011).

Markle, Sandra. *Jackals (Animal Scavengers).* Minneapolis, MN: Lerner (2005).

Learn more online

To learn more about jackals, visit
www.bearportpublishing.com/WildCaninePups

About the author

Jane P. Gardner is a freelance science writer with a master's degree in geology. She worked as a science teacher for several years before becoming a writer. She has written books about science, geography, history, and math.